MAGICAL STORIES FOR CHILDREN

*Fairy Tales Collection with Beautiful Stories
and Great Morals to Help Them to Fall Asleep
Peacefully and Enjoy Sweet Dreams*

Rosa Knight

Table of Contents

INTRODUCTION 6

CHAPTER 1: MR. POT AND MR. KETTLE.............................. 14

CHAPTER 2: TOMMY GETS A NEW FRIEND 20

CHAPTER 3: WHERE ARE YOU? 28

CHAPTER 4: JUST KEEP FISHING 36

CHAPTER 5: GOOD GOOD 44

CHAPTER 6: HOLD ON TO HOPE 52

CHAPTER 7: SARA AND THE EVIL NEIGHBOR......................56

CHAPTER 8: A WEAK SOUL 62

CHAPTER 9: GOOD SPORT 68

CHAPTER 10: WHERE IS YOUR MOTHER? 78

CHAPTER 11: A STICKY SITUATION 86

CONCLUSION 94

Introduction

The fixed daily practice of a bedtime story before resting can improve the child's mental health, language authority, and coherent reasoning skills. The storyteller-audience relationship makes an emotional bond between the parent and the child. Due to "the quality of the imitative intuition" of a child, the parent and the stories that they tell go about as a model for the child to follow.

Bedtime stories are additionally helpful for training the child conceptual excellencies, for example, compassion, benevolence, and discretion, as most children are said to be "normally thoughtful when they have encountered or can envision the feelings of others". Thus, bedtime stories can be utilized to examine darker subjects, for example, passing and racism. As the bedtime stories expand in the topic, the child "will widen in their origination of the lives and feelings of others".

It is never too soon to acquaint your baby with the universe of stories. Specialists recommend that you begin reading them baby stories from an early age to help her imagination. You can do the reading so anyone might hear a habit while you're as yet pregnant, as children perceive their mom's voice in the belly.

Putting time aside to peruse stories consistently is a good habit. Bedtime and naptime are the best times. Making reading a piece of nighttime routine would enable your baby to quiet down and comprehend that it's time to rest. Set the time somewhere close to 6.30 pm and 8.30 pm. whenever after that can make your little one tired.

Bedtime stories are an extraordinary method to improve communication among you and your baby. She will cherish gazing at the brilliant pictures and have specific good time tuning in to the fantasies. Here are various benefits:

1. Creates correspondence:

Story reading helps in the development of children, oral relational abilities, listening capacities, memory, and language acknowledgment skills. It is an excellent method to reinforce her jargon and different sentence structures from an early age.

With time and age, your baby will figure out how to discuss through non-verbal communication, verbal strategies, tuning in, and composed words simply like you.

Children would have heard all the sounds required to communicate in their local language when they turn one. The more you read, the more the child is presented to words.

2. Social and emotional development:

Outlines and stories go connected at the hip, and your baby can create thoughts regarding different toys, creatures, flying creatures, etc. You will discover her utilization of new words to think, feel, and express her feelings.

3. Psychological skills:

Sometime before your baby has begun talking, she is gripping data about the language by tuning in to the stories you read. This will surely receive rewards when your child begins her training.

Children around ten months can figure out how to turn pages and tune in to new words. As your little one keeps on developing, she would take in the specialty of reading from left to right. Infants, who are around a year old, can build up their critical thinking skills by tuning in to bedtime stories.

4. Improves consideration:

Connecting with your baby in bedtime stories is a fantastic method to assist her with getting settled with the reading habit. It is, in fact, a beneficial and sound habit. You can improve her consideration skills by reading to her consistently.

5. Mitigates nervousness:

It is an excellent approach to loosen up her mind and body before hitting the hay. Even if he/she is overstimulated, story reading will assist her with engaging in a completely different world and alleviate from all the tensions.

6. Improves character and information:

As your baby develops, she may fire searching up for specific individuals and draw motivation from them. Reading time is the ideal time to impact the little one and show them life exercises. This can improve her character and information.

7. Turns into a habit:

At the point when you make story-reading your little one's everyday practice, it turns into a habit and a piece of her life. Step by step, reading turns into joy, and you don't need to request that she read after she grows up. Further down the road, the reading may make way for composing.

Tips for Parents:

Try not to make a story reading repetitive to your baby and yourself. Keep it so intriguing that she anticipates this sort of holding with you consistently.

1. Using different feelings and expressive sounds while reading the story encourages the social and emotional development of your baby.

2. As you read, make your child check and answer inquiries to advance social development and thinking skills.

3. Let her mimic sounds, perceive pictures, and learn words.

4. Readout with energy, happiness, and closeness. It encourages them to get related to books.

5. Cuddling while at the same time, reading causes your baby to feel associated, safe, and warm.

6. Sing rhymes and make amusing creature sounds.

7. Don't stress over reading a similar story over and over. Infants cherish and gain from reiteration.

8. Turn off interruptions like TV or radio.

9. By overstating the 'oo' sound in the moon and utilizing words like quiet, you can invigorate associations in the piece of your baby's cerebrum that handles language sounds. The part is known as the sound-related cortex.

10. Remember that the association with your baby is the key to making the most uptime story-reading.

How Stories Feed Imaginations

Each child is brought into the world with imagination, allowing them the chance to envision something that they haven't encountered. A sound imagination is the place inventiveness starts, empowering children to develop into innovative grown-ups. For the children in danger, we serve, inventiveness and critical thinking are essential skills they will require long into their future.

While the world is turning out to be increasingly computerized, a few things don't change. Vis-à-vis storytelling is as yet the foundation of artistic development. This one-on-one association between individuals, bolstered by the story, returns us to the prime example of all training and connections in which one age gives knowledge to the following. However, an excessive number of children pass up the benefits of this trade.

Scientific American reports that children whose parents read to them at bedtime are well on the way to encourage imaginary play conduct. As indicated by clinician Scott Barry Kaufman, taking on different jobs causes them to see different points of view and learn correspondence, critical thinking, and sympathy. Innovative play is related to expanded inventive execution years after the fact, which implies solid imaginations get ready children for increasingly effective and gainful lives. Being an imaginative grown-up doesn't really mean turning into a painter or stone carver either; genuinely, any creative speculation starts with the capacity to envision another reality.

How Healthy Imaginations Make Children More Resilient

Children with progressively created imaginations have a more remarkable capacity to manage pressure and exceptional feelings. Rather than in a split second feeling overpowered, they figure out how to ace their feelings utilizing their imaginations. If a child fears beasts, he can make up a story about chasing down the creature and startling it to transform it into something different. This capacity to self-manage benefits children when they become grown-ups by method for diminished hostility and the ability to endure postponed gratification. Imagination is likewise where children, mainly those we serve, can communicate their true selves. As indicated by specialists, imagination is the place a child can conduct analysis and feel control and force. This is basic for those children who live with tumult or have experienced rehashed affliction.

Significance of reestablishing rest

Reading storybooks over and over enables preschool children to learn words. What's more, dozing soon after learning something extra encourages memory combination and helps to learn in more established children and grown-ups. The present examination investigated how rest advances word learning in preschool children utilizing a common storybook reading task. Children either read a similar story or different stories and either rested after the stories or remained awake. Children's word maintenance was tried 2.5 h later, 24 h later, and after seven days. Results exhibit substantial, diligent impacts for both rehashed readings and rest union on small kids' word learning. A critical finding is that children who read different stories before resting learned words just as children who had the advantage of hearing a similar story. Interestingly, children who read various stories and remained awake never made up for the lost time to their friends on later word learning tests. Suggestions for instructive practices are talked about.

Chapter 1:
Mr. Pot and Mr. Kettle

Mr. Pot and Mr. Kettle were best friends since childhood. They lived in the same house together for twenty years, and they loved each other so much like brothers. One day, the master of the house where they lived fell sick. Several doctors attended to him, but his condition grew worse. Pot and Kettle were very sad. They loved their master so much because he was very kind and nice to them. They didn't want him to die. So, they racked and racked their brains to know what they could do to help him.

After some days of deep thinking, Mr. Pot and Mr. Kettle decided to help their master by getting some healing herbs for him for the next village. So, they went to a hunter who was also their friend.

"Good evening, dear friend," they greeted as soon as they got to his house.

"You are welcome, friends! To what do I owe this pleasurable visit?" he asked them.

"We have come to seek your help, dear friend. Our master is very ill, and we have decided to go to the neighboring village to get some very potent herbs for him. We want to know if we can go with you on your next trip to the village," Mr. Kettle said.

The hunter agreed to help them and take them along with him. He advised them of the kind of herbs they could get for their master. He also told them that the only place they could find such herbs were in the forest and promised to take them along with him.

So, he went into the forest together. In the forest, Mr. Pot, Mr. Kettle, and the hunter searched desperately for those herbal leaves. When they saw a deer, the hunter shot it so that they could also use it to prepare a meal for their master. They went deep into the forest, searching for the herbs. Soon it was evening time, and they had not found anything, and so they were about to give up. Just then, Mr. Kettle looked behind him and saw the herbs they had been searching for. Happily, they took some and headed home.

As soon as they got home, they gave the herbs and deer meat to the cook. The cook went on to do his duties. He used Mr. Pot to prepare a delicious deer meat soup while he used Mr. Kettle to boil the herbs. Mr. Pot got jealous of Mr. Kettle. He wanted to be the one boiling the herbs that would heal their master. But he kept quiet and said nothing. After all, preparations were completed, the cook presented both the meal and the herbs to the master. The master gets well soon after he took the herbs and drank the deer meat soup.

But back in the kitchen, something was brewing up. Mr. Pot and Mr. Kettle were no longer close as they used to be. Mr. Kettle noticed the coldness from Mr. Pot and was worried. So, one day he went to him and said, "my friend, you no longer play with me like before. Have I in any way offended you?" Mr. Pot said nothing in return. He just ignored Mr. Kettle and looked away, pretending as if no one had spoken to him.

When Mr. Kettle saw that Mr. Pot's attitude towards him did not change, he called a family meeting. All the household occupants, the chef, and the master himself were in attendance. As soon as they were seated and well settled, Mr. Kettle spoke, "I welcome every one of you here. I also thank you for honoring my call when I called. May God continue to bless you. Also, I thank God for making our master well again."

"Thank God," they all replied.

Mr. Kettle continued, "I have called you here for a significant reason, to deliberate on a very crucial matter. As you all know, Mr. Pot and I have been best friends for twenty years now, and never have we had a reason to quarrel or separate. But for some time now, I've noticed that my friend, Mr. Pot, has refused to talk to me, let alone play with me. This put me in great distress, and I went to him to ask him what I have done wrong to him, but he refused to give me an answer. He looked away and pretended as if there was no one there talking to him. This is the reason I have called for this meeting so that you can help me ask my best friend here what my offense is."

Everyone was surprised at the story. They began to talk in groups, murmuring to themselves. Then the cook called them to order. "Mr. Pot, you have heard what your friend, Mr. Kettle said. Can you tell us the reason you have decided to ignore your Friend?"

Mr. Pot stood up and said, "thank you, great cook. I greet everyone here today. Thank you for attending."

He looked around him and waited as if waiting for a sign, then he spoke again, "Mr. Kettle is not my friend. In fact, he has never been my friend. All this while, he has been pretending to love me, but I have found out that it is a lie."

"Ah!" everyone screamed in surprise.

Mr. Kettle jumped up. "How can you say that about me? We've been friends since childhood, and now you accuse me of being a pretender," Mr. Kettle said.

There was the noise again as the people continued to murmur.

"Silence!" the master commanded. Silence filled the air again, and the master continued. "Why have you made such accusations, Mr. Pot?"

"Thank you, wise master. When you were sick, Mr. Kettle here and I with our friend, the hunter, went in search of herbs for you so that you could get well. Then we returned to the house after a long day's search. When we returned, the cook used Mr. Kettle to prepare the herbs, which in turn made you well. Mr. Kettle was trying to take the glory of it all forgetting that we both decided to go in search of the herbs together," Mr. Pot replied

"Ah! I never intended to take the glory. This is such a wrong accusation. You are simply jealous," Mr. Kettle replied tearfully.

"Silence," the master said the second time. After they had all kept silent, the master addressed the two friends, Mr. Pot and Mr. Kettle. "Mr. Kettle, it is very wise of you to have called this meeting. Mr. Pot, thank you for caring about me so much. Thank you, Mr. Pot and Mr. Kettle, for taking the time out to search for herbs and also kill a deer for my wellbeing. Indeed, it was a brave and thoughtful decision as it is what helped restore my health. But Mr. Pot, you were good at making soup, were you not? While Mr. Kettle was good at preparing the herbs, isn't it? Don't you know that both you and Mr. Kettle are responsible for my wellbeing? Even if I had taken the herbs and had not taken the soup, I still wouldn't have regained my strength. Both the soup and the herbs worked together to make me well. So, neither you nor Mr. Kettle deserves to take all the glory. But both you, Mr. Pot, and Mr. Kettle deserves to be appreciated because your kindness saved me from that grave illness. So dear Mr. Pot, you have no reason to be jealous of your friend. Moreover, it is only you that can be used to cook soup because of your uniqueness. That is why it is called "a pot of soup" and not a kettle of soup. You have served me well, and you are recognized for your good deeds."

After the master had spoken, Mr. Pot was ashamed of himself for envying his friend. He went to him and apologized for his bad behavior. Mr. Kettle hugged him and accepted him back. The two of them became close friends again, and nothing ever came in between them again. They lived together and loved each other for the rest of their lives.

Chapter 2:
Tommy Gets A New Friend

Tommy was an ace in the water. He had been swimming and snorkeling since he was a toddler. His Dad took him down to the sea when he was a newborn and held him in his arms while he walked up and down the beach, talking to his new son. Something had happened in those early times that Tommy could not quite grasp, but he knew one thing for sure. He loved the ocean; he loved everything about it. The white sands, the blue water, and what could be out there in the deeps? He did not know, but he was going to find out, and now he had a much better understanding of how that would take shape. Dragons!

Tommy had brought his snorkeling gear and was sitting up against the rocks, getting ready to go into the water, when he heard a sound in his head. "Hello, Tommy!" It was baby Drake, and Tommy was thrilled. Meeting Drake was the first meaningful psychic conversation he had experienced, and he was excited to learn more about his powers and the strange new creature who had come up from the depths to meet him, or so he thought.

"Is that you, Drake? Where are you?" Tommy mentally asked. "Still full of questions, I see." Drake replied and, "I am out at the end of the point. Is anyone there around you, or on the beach near where you are?" Drake asked. Tommy looked around but saw no one. "I am here at the point, and I do not see anyone," Tommy informed Drake. "Okay, then I'm coming in." was all that the little dragon said. It wasn't long before Tommy saw him again. He came up out of the water very near to where Tommy was sitting and walked across the sand to sit beside his new friend.

"You may ask any questions you have now," the dragon said. "Thank you," Tommy said and began to think of what to ask and how to word the questions so as not to make the testy little guy angry again. He began. "Do you have parents, and where do you live?" Tommy asked. "Yes, and we live not far from here on the bottom, in a large cave that is filled with air. The cave is an ancient and sacred place that we dragons have been visiting for centuries, and my Mother and Father live there, as well as my two older sisters. Would you like to meet them?" Drake asked. All this was nearly too much for little Tommy, so he thought for a moment and then gathered his wits and began to speak. "I would be honored to meet your family if they would have me." this was all he said. "Good, very good, my friend," said the little dragon.

They talked for a good hour before both going into the water to swim. Tommy swam down into the shallows of the lagoon, and Drake was there right beside him. Drake found exciting things, and Tommy picked them up, and they went back up and onto the beach to check out their artifacts. This they did for the next three hours, and Tommy found his new friend to be a great company. They found some old plates, and an old rusty lantern, and something else that was mostly buried that they could not pull out of the sea bottom. Tommy told Drake that he would bring something to dig with tomorrow, and they said goodbye for the day, and Tommy headed home.

That night, Tommy awakened suddenly to voices in his head. He could not determine what it was or why he was hearing them, and eventually, he fell back asleep. In the morning, like all mornings, breakfast with his Mom and Dad, and then back to the beach, only this time, he brought a small camping shovel.

Much to his surprise, there was Drake, sitting upon a rock sunning himself.

"Good morning Tommy," Drake said. "Hi there, Mr. Dragon," Tommy responded.

"Did you hear us talking last night?" Drake asked. "Yes, I did. So that was you, after all. I wondered about that." Tommy said, mentally to Drake. "Why did I hear you, but you were not talking directly to me?" Tommy asked. "Oh that," Drake said, looking down at the rocks. "Well, actually, I'm new at this psychic stuff, and I was talking to my parents, and it just sorts of slipped out. I kinda turned it on by mistake, so you really were not supposed to hear any of that, but no matter."

Drake replied. "You know, I was worried about the very same thing," Tommy said to Drake. "I guess there is no rule book for this psychic communication stuff is there?" Tommy stated, and "Well, I know one thing for sure, and that is, if I am mindful, my thoughts should be just my own. What I mean to say is that nobody else should be able to hear my thoughts, right?" Tommy said.

"Drake," Tommy suddenly said, "I want to talk to you about something. You are a tiny dragon, and I am a tiny human, so I guess we are both kinds of in the same boat if you know what I mean. What I want to say is that my parents have always taken me to church on Sunday mornings. Always! I mean, we never miss church. I think it has always meant a lot to them, but anyhow this church is not exactly like a normal church. I mean, we pray and read the Bible and sing hymns, but there is much more to it. They have classes that my parents have always made me go to after each service that teach something sort of different than other churches do. It is called mindful meditation. Have you ever heard of that?" Tommy asked the dreary eyed little dragon. "Wow, that was a mouthful you just said. No, I can't say I've ever heard of mindful meditation, but we practice fire breathing. Is it anything like that?" Drake asked.

Tommy burst out laughing and thought the little Dragon was only kidding. Drake's eyes became really huge, and he made a sort of gurgling growling sound deep down in his throat. "Uh, Oh, did I make you mad?" Tommy asked. "Well, it sounded like you thought that a huge part of my life was funny!" Drake snarled. "Oh, no-no-no," Tommy quickly snapped. "Really, I just thought you were…. Uh, well, I guess I wasn't listening right, that must be it. So, tell me more about this fire breathing thing you do then." Tommy gasped. He didn't want to lose his only friend, and certainly didn't want to be on the receiving end of a burst of flames!

"Well, we dragons by nature have certain abilities, and that is one of them. I guess you could say it would be a little bit like our ability to use mental communication. I think the off worlders call that telepathy." A more calm Drake stated. Just then, a group of tourists could be seen clambering up the jetty from the other side. Since Drake had his back to the jetty, he didn't see them. "Quick, back in the water. Somebody is coming!" Tommy gasped, whereby the little dragon dove headlong into the shallows near the jetty. As the tourists appeared in full force upon the jetty, Tommy waved hello to them, hoping they had not caught sight of the dragon.

The situation returned to normal, the tourists faded out of sight down the beach, and Drake's head bobbed up some distance out in the water. Tommy just beckoned to him and then noticed the dragon moving closer to him. "That was close." The dragon said, and "I don't like being spotted by strangers, as you may recall from the odd meeting on the fishing boat." Tommy chuckled and said, "I think that was planned actually, don't you?" he asked. "Okay my friend, I guess you already know that we wanted to make contact with you, is that what you are thinking then?" Drake asked. "Well, I am just glad you did because you know I have these abilities, these powers, and I'm just a kid of 9, so I'm still sorting everything out myself," Tommy explained.

The two chatted for another hour, and then agreed to meet the next day again; same time, the same place. "Good, Okay then see you tomorrow Drake," Tommy said, and with that, the little dragon again dove into the shallows and was gone. Tommy sat there thinking for a good deal of time after Drake left. He was putting together a plan in his mind as to how to learn more about all this. He would have to run it by the dragon tomorrow. With that, Tommy picked up his things and rode home.

The evening was mundane, and Tommy went to bed, but he could not stop thinking about Drake. He thought that just maybe he would "call" Drake up with his mind and say goodnight. Yes, he thought, that would be an experiment for me so I can figure this telepathy thing out. Tommy used his mindfulness and cleared his thoughts. Then, he did some meditation and used his third eye technique to calm himself even further. After that, in his mind, he said, "Drake, can you hear me?" Boom! Just like magic, Drake was there in his mind. "Hi Tommy, how are you?" Drake said. "Just wanted to reach out and say thanks for meeting me today." Tommy thought. "Sure, no problem, it was fun. We'll talk again tomorrow. Good night." The dragon said, and "Good night, my friend, until tomorrow then." And with that, Tommy signed off. That was easy, Tommy thought. "I guess it's just all about mindfulness and meditation, isn't it?" Tommy thought to himself and then fell into a deep sleep.

Chapter 3:
Where Are You?

Iggy was a shy little iguanodon. He was very small and had bright green skin. He walked along, close to the ground, and often using his fingers to help him take his steps. But, he was also able to stand up on two legs to reach leaves that were higher up on the trees. He was not very big yet—he still had a lot of growing to do, but he could still just barely start to reach up to some of the lower leaves.

Iggy, as shy as he was, loved to spend all of his time with his mother. He loved her dearly and loved nothing more than to be with her whenever he could be. He followed her around as much as he could, and he cried every time she left him at the nest to go and take care of something else. He wanted to stay with her forever, but sometimes, that was just not possible, and he knew that. But, that didn't stop him from wishing it was so.

One day, when his mother went out to collect food and asked him to stay put at his home, Iggy felt sad. He was not happy to spend his time alone, and he did not want to stay at home without anyone else there, mainly because he could see some great, big clouds in the distance that looked like they were bringing with them a big storm. Just the thought of a storm and thunder and lightning made a shiver run down his spine, and he didn't want anything to do with it. "Maybe I should go and find my mother," he finally told himself, hopping out of his nest and looking off into the distance, where he remembered she had headed.

And with that, Iggy decided to be on his way. He knew that he would find her! He just had to keep on going the right direction, and he would run into her eventually, surely, he told himself. And off, he went with his little iguanodon feet. He let himself begin to relax, trusting that before long, he would be reunited with his mother and safe from harm!

Before long, he ran into a little old Euoplocephalus. "What are you doing?" she asked him in a quiet voice that wavered with age. "You're young to be wandering about on your own, aren't you, laddie?" She squinted her eyes, and Iggy was pretty sure that she could not see very well. He did not blame her either— she was awfully old, after all.

"I'm off to find my mother," he said.

"Oh, she left you?" asked the Euoplocephalus.

"No, no!" Iggy replied. "I was left at my nest to wait for her… But I got scared and went looking for her. He sighed. He was starting to feel scared again already. He thought that he would find her by then for sure, but she was nowhere to be found! He would have to look high and low to find her, and he did not know where to get started. He looked all around him but did not have much luck at all, and that was very disappointing to him.

"I see," said the Euoplocephalus. "Maybe you should just go home and wait there!" She nodded her head a few times as if agreeing with herself. "It would be for your own good, after all. What good is it for you to be lost in the middle of nowhere? And what if she goes back to the nest and you aren't there? She would be petrified, you know."

Iggy shook his head. "If she were going home, she'd walk this way," he replied. "She would have to go past me, and that means that she would not miss me at all. I just have to make sure that I keep going until I run into her."

"What if she turns somewhere or gets off track?" asked the Euoplocephalus. "Then, she won't still be right on this trail at all."

"No, she would have to go past me!" Iggy said stubbornly, shaking his own head back and forth. "She has to walk this way, or she will miss going home!"

The elderly dinosaur shrugged her shoulders. It wasn't her problem to figure out, she supposed, but she didn't want to start a fight either. Besides, it was hardly her place to tell someone else's child what to do, so she simply turned to get going. "Good luck, and stay safe."

Iggy nodded his head. "Thank you!" he called out to her as he kept on traveling along the road. Hopefully, he told himself, he would be able to find her soon, and all of this would no longer matter. That would be the perfect scenario, and he would be thrilled to see that happen.

Of course, things were not always that simple, and sometimes, other complications had to be faced. As Iggy continued to walk, following the scent of his mother as he did so, the rain started to fall. It fell drop by drop until suddenly, it was pouring down rain! The rain was so steady and so heavy that Iggy realized it would wash away the scent he was following! He would not be able to use it to keep following his mother!

"That's okay!" he eventually told himself. "I can just follow in her footsteps since I can see them on the ground." And so, he did. He followed along, humming to himself and putting each foot into the footprints as he went. He imagined that he was big and strong and able to follow his mother anywhere! He imagined that he was a great, big grownup iguanodon and that he would be able to go anywhere that he wanted and eat any of the leaves he dreamed about. As he walked along in his daydream, he had a great, big grin on his face.

But soon, there was a big flash of lightning and a great, big crash of thunder! It was so loud that Iggy felt it shake up his entire body, and he jumped up and looked around, realizing that he had gotten pretty far without paying attention. He looked down at the ground, and his mother's footprints had been washed away by the rain, and when he tried to think about where he was, he realized something scary.

Iggy was lost.

"Mama?" he called out, but the rain and the thunder were too loud. "Mama, where are you?" he called again. He felt his eyes starting to water, but he did not want to cry. "Mama! Mama!" he cried out just as another great, big crash of thunder shook the area. The storm was right above him now, and it was kind of scary. He looked all around him but could not figure out where he was going or how he should even start to get home. It was hard to really figure that out when he didn't know where he was that moment. All he knew was that he was scared.

He walked around sadly, looking left and right. He could not find any signs that would help him recognize where he was or how he could get home. "Hello?" he cried out every now and then, but the only answer he got back was the sound of the pouring rain. Before long, the little dinosaur was very cold, very wet, and very miserable. He just wanted to go home and cuddle his Mama, but he could not figure out the right way to get where he needed to go. Soon, he gave up. He threw himself down on the ground in defeat and let the rain wash over him. Maybe he'd keep trying after the storm...

"You're still out here?"

The voice surprised Iggy, and when he turned around, there was that very same old Euoplocephalus standing there in the rain. The water bounced off of her hardback, and she didn't seem to mind the rain at all. "You're lost, aren't you?" she asked him, her voice kind.

"Yes…" Iggy replied sadly, looking down. Maybe he should have stayed home after all.

"Come with me, little one," said the Euoplocephalus. "Auntie, Ellie will take you home."

Auntie, Ellie turned out to be very patient, and she carefully and calmly guided Iggy home. Every time that Iggy got scared, she was right there to help. Any time that Iggy tripped or fell, Auntie Ellie helped him get up and helped move him over and get him right back up on his feet. She was quite old, but she still moved with enough strength to help the poor, young, frightened Iguanodon make his way through the storm.

Soon, Iggy began to recognize where they were. He began to see things that looked familiar and places that he was confident he knew. He saw great, big trees that he knew that he would eat from—he could see the markings from his Mama's claws. He saw the rock that he liked to climb up and jump off of. He saw the stream that he usually played in. "We're almost home!" he told Auntie Ellie. "How did you know?"

Auntie Ellie smiled. "I just had a good feeling," she said to him with a little nuzzle. All of the iguanodons lived in that area, and she was very certain that he probably would, too, and so she had brought him all the way there.

Then, Iggy saw her—his mother was sitting in their nest, looking very worried. When she saw him, she came running toward him. "Iggy!" she cried out.

"Mama!" he called back.

"What were you thinking? I was so scared!" She nuzzled Iggy and picked him up in one quick scoop, looking over and under him to make sure he was okay, and he was. He was just covered in mud and would need a good cleaning. Iggy was thrilled to be back with his mother, but he was tired, too. As his Mama thanked Auntie Ellie over and over again for bringing him home safely, Iggy cuddled up against her. He was feeling very, very sleepy, and he was sure that, before long, he would be fast asleep...

Iggy learned a fundamental lesson that day. He learned that going out when his mother told him that he needed to stay put was never a good idea. He learned that he owed it to her to listen and that when his mother told him something, it was because she loved him and she wanted him to stay safe, so he needed to listen to what she had to say. And with that lesson learned, he never wandered off again.

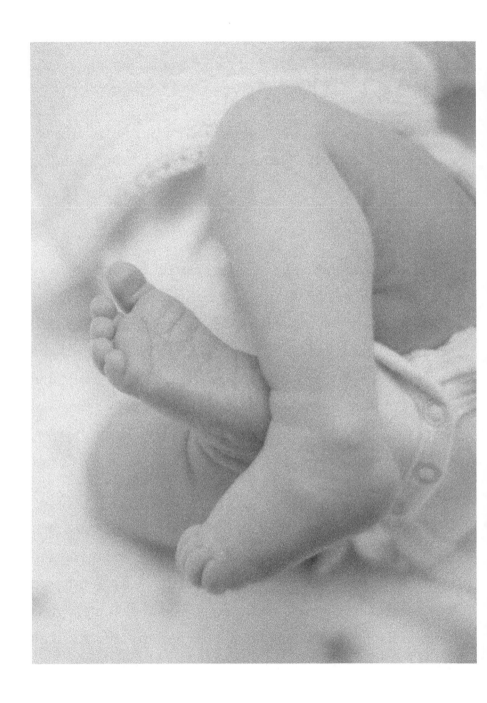

Chapter 4:
Just Keep Fishing

L ong, long ago, near a great big river, there lived a spinosaurus family. Spinosaurus had a long, skinny jaw, a great, big sail on their back, and a wide, flat tail that is used to help it swim quickly through the water. It stood on two big legs with long claws on the toes, and its hands were little, with three claws for grasping on each one. Spinosaurus was a swimming dinosaur, and it was built to be able to swim right through the water with ease. It was built to be able to splash and swim and catch all sorts of yummy fish to eat within its long jaws.

The spinosaurus family that lived by the river had a mom, a dad, a big brother named Sven, and a little sister named Selah. Sven and Selah liked each other enough. They would play all day if they had to. They would spend time together. But, Sven liked to leave Selah all alone so he could go diving for fish. He loved to find himself some yummy snacks that he could enjoy when they were out playing, especially because he knew that he would need the practice for when he was older. He knew that if he were not careful, he would never be able to go out on his own to learn to fish, and that scared him, so he practiced every chance he got.

Selah, on the other hand, did not like the water much. Selah did not like the idea of going underwater, and she did not like using her tail to move throughout it, even though that was what she was built for. She knew that she was born to swim, but she did not like it one bit. She would do everything in her power to avoid getting in the water, and when she had to go in, she found that she could never catch a fish. She was too slow. She was too loud. Sometimes, she was simply unlucky and could not find a single fish to chase after! She would try and try when her parents would bother her too, but she felt like she had other things to do instead, especially because she was so bad at fishing. Instead of swimming, she told herself, she could try building something. She could make things for other dinosaurs. She could babysit other dinosaurs. She could even try taking the time to do other things instead. She didn't care what she had to do, so long as it was not fishing because she knew that, no matter how hard she tried, she would never be good at it. Her mother and father were natural fishers. Even Sven was a natural fisher! But, Selah, on the other hand, struggled ever to catch even a minnow. Something that she did just never worked for her, no matter how hard she tried.

One day, when Selah and Sven were at the river, Selah watched as Sven dove in and out of the water with ease. She watched as he fished up fish after fish after fish, tossing a few her way, too.

"You sure you don't want to come in?" called her brother. "I can teach you if you want to."

Selah shook her head back and forth. "I don't want to!" she said stubbornly, and she meant it. She did not want to learn how to fish at all. She simply wanted to spend her time doing her own thing and playing her own games, if it was the last thing that she could do. She set off quietly on the shore, watching how well her brother dove in and out of the water, wishing that she could do it, too.

Selah scooted closer to the water and dipped just one toe into it. It was chilly! She watched her brother dart around back and forth, with the fish on the shore very quickly piling up. She smiled sadly.

Of course, dreams were just that—dreams—and Selah was not going to hold her breath, waiting around for it to happen magically. She needed to make her dreams happen if she really wanted them at all, and she knew that. But, she had no idea what she would have to do to make them happen in the first place other than just try.

"Big brother?" Selah called out, and the bigger spinosaurus stopped to look at her.

"What is it?" he called back.

"I want to fish."

"Really?" he replied.

"Yes," she answered. She was not wholly convinced of the position, but she knew that if she wanted to be able to be big and strong and able to take care of herself, she had to learn to do it herself, and that was something that she wanted. She wanted to be her dinosaur. She wanted to be able to do her own thing whenever it mattered instead of being stuck. She wanted to be able to live on her own when she was bigger without needing to keep her family's health. She wanted to be able to fish up her food all by herself, and she knew that with the right kind of training, she could make it happen...

She was just afraid to do so.

Sven seemed excited about the idea of teaching Selah how to fish. He nodded his head and swam to shore. "Okay," he told his sister. "To begin, you must start by getting good at swimming, you know. That means that you have to work hard to swim all around the water, no matter the current. You need to be able to keep yourself moving if you want to be able to chase after the fish, and that is really difficult to get right if you are not practicing a lot. Can you do it?"

Selah nodded her head. "Of course!" she said, but she was not so convinced. But, she slid into the water, even knowing that she doubted herself. She climbed right in, eager to make a great, big splash and eager to prove to the whole wide world that she knew what she was doing and she knows how to fish. Her body was designed to let her slide right through the water, and that was exactly what she did. With every pump of her powerful tail, she was able just to glide through.

"Great," called out Sven, watching as she swam from place to place. He swam with her, quicker than she was, but not really trying to race. "Now, try to catch a fish!" He looked around and then pointed at one that was not too far away. "Get that one. All you have to do is get close enough to the fish to... Grab it!" and right after he said grab it, he lunged forward and managed to snatch up the fish in his jaws with ease. It took him no effort at all, and the fish was in his mouth, gobbled down, and swallowed in the blink of an eye.

Selah was nervous. How could she ever possibly do that, too? She was not convinced that she could, and yet, she knew that she had to try. She did her best, pushing herself to swim further and faster, and as soon as she saw a fish that looked promising, she tried to swim as quickly as she could. But, as she swam quickly, the fish must have heard her coming, as it suddenly disappeared into the watery kelp beds below. It is challenging to catch a fish with your jaws, after all.

When the fish disappeared, Selah sighed as she lifted her head out of the water. She was really hoping that she would get lucky and catch the first fish! But, of course, that did not happen at all.

"Keep trying!" her brother called out, and Selah nodded. He had no trouble catching a few more fish while Selah swam around, trying. Every time she would start to swim forward, she splashed a little bit too much, and the fish would then leave. It did not want to get eaten!

They kept trying, again and again, and Selah was starting to get tired. No matter how hard she tried and no matter how often she pumped her tail behind her or how quickly she tried to move, the fish was always just out of reach.

"You know," her brother said, watching her thoughtfully. "I think that the problem is that you are splashing too much." He looked at her tail as she swam about, to and fro. "You make your tail go up and down a little bit, but that slows you down, and it changes the way that you are swimming. I think it may also be giving the fish a warning before they need a warning, and they are using that warning to escape. If you were to fix that, I think you may have a chance at catching them!"

Selah nodded her head slowly. That made sense, she thought... if the problem was that she was swimming too slowly or she was splashing in a way that told the fish that she was coming, of course, they would run away. They want not to get eaten just like all other animals, so of course, they disappear when they saw Selah going their way. But, if Selah changed the way that she moved her tail, she would stop making that splash entirely.

"I'm not sure I can do it," she finally told her brother.

"Of course you can," he replied without a doubt in the world. "Just try. For me?"

The littler spinosaurus nodded her head. She really didn't want to, but for her brother... she would do anything. With a sigh and thinking about what her brother said and how he had to move, she practiced moving her tail without splashing. It was hard at first, but her brother helped her learn to line her tail just right, and soon, it was easy! She started to pick up on it!

"I think you're ready," said Sven, setting her up and looking for the first fish that he wanted her to chase after. It did not take long for that first fish to swim past. "Go!"

And off Selah went, swimming as quickly as she could. Her tail swung back and forth, and she opened up her jaws, and.... She caught the fish! She did it! She had managed to get one without struggling so much! It was all because she had listened to her brother! Even though she was afraid to fish and she was worried that she would struggle to do so, she had done it! All she had to do was keep trying, even when she was done and even when she was convinced that she would not be able to make it happen!

And so, Selah learned that it was very important always to work hard to try to do something meaningful. She learned that working harder and working on trying to do everything that she needed on her own and with help was better than giving up, and she learned that if she really tried hard not to give up, she would be able to succeed!

Chapter 5:
Good Good

F
ar, far away, there lived a stegosaurus named Rocco. Rocco, the stegosaurus, had lots of high, prominent spines on his back that helped to protect him. Most of them were bigger than his head, and they were very good protection against dinosaurs like T-rex, who sometimes wanted to take a bite of Stegosaurus meat. Rocco was still quite young, and his spikes were not very big yet. He was old enough to be away from his mother and father, but still young enough to be done growing.

Like all living things, Rocco loved to eat. He loved to find all sorts of tasty food, and he was always willing to travel far and wide to make sure that he got it, no matter what it took and no matter where it was. He would climb up mountains to get food. He would travel over rivers and lakes with rafts for food. He would find good food and eat them out of gardens that other dinosaurs grew in their free time. Sometimes, he would even go out of his way to find other areas that would have all sorts of delicious options for him, so he did not have to eat the same thing over and over again.

Rocco would tell anyone who asked that he was the king of cuisine—he made it his mission to go around and try as much food as he could. He never wanted to eat the same thing so much that it got boring, and so, that was what he did with his time.

Everyone else had a different word for Rocco—**picky.** They always called him picky. His mother would always tell him that food has a purpose—it feeds you to give you energy. "It goes in one end, and it comes out the other!" his mother would say. "Who cares what it is when it all ends up the same?" But, Rocco thought that if he is feeding something to his body, it better be the best food that he can give himself. That is the best way to make sure that he can, in fact, be healthy! Of course, he was picky with his food—he wanted it to be not only nutritious, but also tasty, too, and that meant no silly foods like those weeds that his mother would normally pick and bring back to the nest. No more low-growing grasses and bushes! Rocco was on a mission, and that mission was to find the greatest food he ever could!

One day, Rocco was walking about. He was in the mountains that day, searching for something that would be just right for his breakfast. He didn't want it to be something like weeds or grass that day; he was hoping for something sweet, tasty, and maybe even just a little bit different than normal. He was thinking about beautiful red berries and some mushrooms, all mixed with some delicate greens into a wonderful salad...

And he was thinking about it so much that he didn't realize that there was someone in front of him! He walked right into an elderly Euoplocephalus, who did not seem to be bothered very much at all by his presence. "I'm very sorry!" Rocco said, bowing his head with a sheepish grin.

"Oh, nonsense!" said the old Euoplocephalus. "That was all Auntie Ellie's fault! Don't say sorry at all! But, I must say... You look absolutely famished. Have you been eating enough, dearie? Did you get all of the food that you needed? Do you need anything else today? I happen to have some great mushrooms back in my nest..."

"Mushrooms?" asked Rocco. "Really?"

"Of course, my dear!" said Auntie Ellie. She was the area's local elderly dinosaur who sort of adopted all of the younger generations as her own, in a way. She loved to spoil all of the younger ones, usually in return for a little bit of help to make sure that everything was getting done. She couldn't always move the rocks around as much as she used to, and sometimes, she needed some young blood to help. "They're some wonderful mushrooms that I gathered, but they still need—"

"Berries?" Rocco chimed in excitedly, hoping that she was indeed thinking about berries that they would be able to enjoy together.

"You got it!" she replied with a grin. "My, doesn't that sound delicious?"

"Yeah!" Rocco replied. "You won't believe it—I was actually out here looking or berries and mushrooms for food for today! It sounded amazing, and I was really hoping that I would be able to find them—and sure enough, here you are!" He grinned at her.

"What a wonderful coincidence!" replied Auntie Ellie. She seemed genuinely excited to have a guest that had the same taste in food as she did, and she was glad to have someone around that would be able to help them all. "Well, let's get looking then!"

Rocco nodded. "Do you know where the berries grow?"

"Of course I do, dearie!" replied Auntie Ellie.

"Where?" Rocco asked excitedly. He had always wanted to know where they were. But, Auntie Ellie grinned. "I can't give away all of my secrets yet, now can I?

Rocco had to admit; she did have a very good point! If she told him where the berries grew, she might not have enough for herself, too! Besides, the food would always taste better when the work was done for it, so Rocco was not going to be deterred just by that! He was determined to find the food himself, and he knew that he could do it if he put his mind to it!

So, off Rocco went, searching for that elusive bush of yummy red berries. They were sweet and round and very large, and they were usually surrounded by all sorts of bugs that were attracted by the smell. He looked high and low, although he was quite slow, thanks to his size. He had to take it one step at a time, peeking underneath plants and looking all around him.

Soon, Rocco found something! It was a great, big tree with fruits growing on it, but he could not quite see the color. He went over to it as quickly as his bumbling legs could take him. Before long, he was standing right next to a great tree! The tree had what looked like red berries stuck to it, but he could not reach them. He tried standing up taller, with his front legs balancing on the tree's trunk, but he still could not reach! He was too small!

He tried looking down at the ground, but the only berries that were already down there looked kind of sad. They were starting to dry, and most of them had strange dents in them that made it very clear that they were supposed to be processed better. They looked terrible, and the smell was even worse! But, he was sure that those were the fresh berries that he was looking for. He just had to figure out how to get them down.

He could throw something at the tree, he thought briefly. That should shake up the tree trunk enough to drop some berries to gather up! But, when he threw the only rock that he could find nearby that was actually big enough compared to the rock, nothing happened. Rocco frowned. "Well. That didn't work," the stegosaurus told himself. But, something was bound to work eventually! He just had to figure out what it was that he had to do! So, he tried something else instead. He tried standing up taller. Maybe he could use his feet to kick it until some berries fell off, but the first kick was enough to make the tree start to crash—and then fall to the ground.

Rocco felt a bit bad; he kicked the tree enough to break it when really, all he wanted was the berries. He leaned forward and took a nibble at one—and promptly spat it out. Those weren't the right berries! The right berries had to be around there somewhere—he just had to find it! So, off he went, searching as much as he could to find the right berry bush that would have what he needed, pretending that he did not just accidentally knock down an entire tree.

Soon, Rocco came to a bush. This bush was much closer to the ground—so close, in fact, it seemed to be mostly ignored by the other animals that were alive. It was a bright green bush with stiff leaves and dotted with little red berries all over it. The berries looked tasty. They smelled tasty. And, sure enough, Rocco could hear lots of insects buzzing about. Maybe this was the right berry. He took a bite of the berries, only to find that it was, in fact, delicious. They were exactly the right kind of berries for what he wanted to do! He just had to get them all back to where he wanted them, and that wouldn't be too much of a problem—at least, he hoped it wouldn't. He picked up several branches of berries and carried them back to Auntie Ellie's nest, hoping that she would have a great way to combine everything.

When he arrived back at her nest, she was overjoyed. "Those are exactly right, my dearie!" she told him with a grin, and she took the berries that he had brought and mixed them together in a carefully constructed stone bowl. The berries were mashed into a mix and then combined with chunks of onions and then cooked them all. The food smelled amazing, and there was even a little bowl filled up with garden greens, too! It looked like they would be having some of the greatest food ever, and Rocco was thrilled. It was absolutely worth the effort based on the smell. And, when it was all done cooking, he was very happy to get to eat it!

"Thank you," he told Auntie Ellie with a grin as he waited for the food to cool down. He looked at the wonderful dish that she made, and he was more excited than he had been in a very long time. He was ready to chow down as soon as the temperature was low enough, and he was so excited about getting to try those flavors.

Rocco learned that it is important always to help out when you want something; he was happy to help with what needed to be done, and he was happy to share in the work that had to happen, in return for getting the food. He had no problems at all, making that happen and enjoying the food as well, and he was very excited to try again in the future. If he could help Auntie Ellie every day to find some food for their supper every day, he would gladly do so.

Chapter 6:
Hold on to Hope

In the past time, there was a beautiful and kind-hearted unicorn called Angelica, and she had a single son who lived with her the most beautiful and memorable moments in her life; he was the best thing that she had in her life.

She loved him very much and took care of him, their lives were full of happiness and contentment, even her son was polite and obedient, and he never disobeyed her orders.

One day this son's destiny was bad, and he died after a sudden accident. It was a complete shock to her.

At that time, Angelica was deeply saddened by the death of her only son, her heart broke into small pieces, and she lived with great misery for a long time until she lost that luster that characterizes the unicorns from any other creatures.

Despite this, hope remained and did not despair, as she believes that there must be a way to bring her son back to life.

So she went to one of the witches in the village, and she told her the story in detail, and that she is ready to apply anyway to bring her son back to life.

She said: Listen, witch, my son is the whole world for me, and I think that his death was the result of my negligence, I cannot live since he died, can you help me to restore him? I will do anything.

The witch thought a lot about the what mother said, and she replied with compassion and sympathy: I can give you a good solution, I think that it may bring your son back to life, but this is on the condition that you bring me an apple seed from a house where no one has ever felt sad.

Mother Angelica rejoiced at the witch's response to her; she felt that there's hope, and she can see her son again.

She went to every home in the village, looking for her goal. She knocked on the first door, a pale unicorn opened for her, she was young, but her appearance suggests sadness.

Angelica asked her: Dear, I am looking for a house that where no one has ever felt sad, can you help me if you have never grieved you and your family before? I only need an apple seed.

The weak unicorn invited Angelica to enter the house with a light smile, she said in pain: Did my home ever know anything but sorrow? At first, my husband passed away two years ago, and since then my life is becoming black by little, he passed and left three little unicorns that I have to take care of, and I work so hard to provide them with a living every day, I even sold a lot of our furniture to get food for my children. However, I am content and satisfied with my life, and I am proud of it, I firmly stand in the face of hardship.

Mother Angelica sympathized with her a lot and told her: You have such a beautiful soul and healthy heart. Can you consider me as a friend of yours from today? I will be very honored.

Both agreed to become friends to relieve each other after the confused mother ended her long visit at the first house, she entered another house to ask about the same request.

The house owner, who was a strong young unicorn told her: My husband is very sick and his horn breaks over time, how can I not be sad about him? I had to work in tough jobs to provide food for him and our children, but I do not complain, I will continue to care for my husband and children as long as I live and I will provide them with everything they need.

Mother Angelica immediately set up and decided to help this strong unicorn; she went to the market to buy food for her, her children, and her sick husband.

She said goodbye to her warmly, she said: I was really honored to know you, and do not consider this food as compassion or charity, please consider it as a gift of our friendship, I also met another great unicorn a little while ago, I will introduce you to her later. Please, take care of yourself, and if you needed anything, I would always be there for you.

The mother left the second house and started entering a house after a house, looking for the happy one among them, but all her attempts were unsuccessful.

However, it is worth noting that this mother was kind to the families of all the houses that she entered, and she tried to help every house to relieve their grief, by supporting them with their needs as much as possible.

With the passage of days, Angelica became a friend of all the village houses, and this led to her that she completely forgot her goal, which is to search for the apple seed from any happy house that did not feel depression or sadness.

The mother became involved in the problems of others, forgetting her sorrow without realizing that the witch had cooperated with her to give her much better and stronger way to end her sadness, even if she did not find the apple seed that she was looking for, and even if she did not bring her son back to life, that witch gave her friends and gave her the conviction.

Angelika said to herself: I am not the only one who suffers in this world, because we all suffer from difficulties and crises, because life is just like this, it does not go in one way, we will go through good days and we must also go through bad days. What should we do in bad days and painful accidents? Just be patient and stand in solidarity with one another, and wait for those good days to come again, and they will surely come back.

Chapter 7:
Sara and the Evil Neighbor

One rainy day in the winter, one of the most beautiful unicorns ever was born, she was characterized by breathtaking and unusual features, her parents were flying very high from the intensity of their happiness, they called her Sara, and they wished only one thing and that they can bring her up properly so that her morals become as beautiful as her appearance.

Our little girl grew up between the arms of a happy quiet family, her father was simple in his appearance and lifestyle, but he enjoyed a great amount of wisdom and intelligence.

Her mother was very loving, and all she wanted in life was that her beautiful daughter Sara could grow up, and become the best and most beautiful unicorn in the whole town.

But this happiness was lacking something; the parents noticed that their dear daughter did not have her two wings yet, while all of her friends had beautiful and colorful wings.

They waited for another period hoping that she would grow two wings, but no use, they went to more than one doctor, but they all could not solve the problem.

One day her mother was sitting with one of her neighbors, she was called Julia, the neighbor said: Unfortunately, with all this beauty and attraction, your daughter is without wings, she will miss the one thing that makes unicorns special creatures, I think her beauty will not be useful now. Fortunately, my daughter has two large and beautiful wings, she is a complete unicorn, and she will not feel the suffering as your daughter.

Sara's mother felt very sad. Julia's words hurt her and diminished her daughter in front of her. Thus she said: My daughter is still young, her wings are only late, but she will definitely have two wings, and you know what? Even if her two wings did not grow, I will remain proud of her and remain faithful that she is a complete unicorn and even the most beautiful unicorn in this town. I know that you do not love my daughter and that you are bothered by the great admiration of people for her and their neglect of your daughter because they were born on the same day.

Julia felt angered and shouted: My daughter will always be better than your fluffy daughter.

Then she left and closed the door forcefully behind her, the mother cried, and she could not control herself, she knows that her daughter is being bullied and ridiculed by her peers, but at the same time, she did not know what to do.

She went to every doctor in the town, but no one could help her, and at once, she heard about a sage in the town, people say about him that he has a solution to any problem.

Sara's mother took her daughter and went to him; his appearance seemed like a magician. They sat in front of him with a bit of fear.

The mother started to speak: All her friends are learning to fly while she stands alone to see them from the ground. My friends bully her just in front of me, and I can do nothing but cry.

The magician noticed something and quickly said: What do your friends say?

She answered: They say that Sara is famous and well-liked, but she is not a complete unicorn, and that their daughters are complete ones, and that they are more worthy of fame and love than my daughter.

The magician calmly approached the little unicorn, looked deeply in her pretty brown eyes and then said with dismay: They made a curse on your daughter to prevent the growth of her wings, I do not know how could unicorns do such evil things, we are nice and peaceful beings who do not like evil and harmful actions.

The mother said as hope began to know a way to her sad heart: How can we remove this curse? I am ready to do whatever it takes.

He told her in shock: It is not possible, only the unicorn who threw the curse on your daughter should want it to disappear, only then the curse shall disappear, and your daughter shall grow two wings, if that does not happen then she will never have wings, I fear that I can do nothing more than that to help you, I am very sorry.

The mother's heart was broken when she heard this news. How can she know who made this? Even if she knew, how can she persuade whoever made this curse to remove it?

She spent long nights thinking about it and asked more than a friend, she even asked some of her neighbors, but she did not find any answer to give her a solution.

One day the wingless little girl walked in a narrow street, the street was empty, but after a few steps, she heard a sound of screaming.

Sara dashed towards the sound to find the arrogant unicorn who had argued with her mother several days ago, Julia, whose wings were stuck in a pile of wood that she fell on while flying.

She tried to come up with help, but she did not find any unicorns around, she wanted to help her, but she was at a great height, she tried to jump for her, but no use, and suddenly the stuck unicorn said: Well well, I am removing the curse.

Suddenly, the little girl grew two big wings, she froze in her place from her amazement, but soon she woke up to the sound of repeated distress.

Beautiful Sara flew for the first time in her life, she wanted to fly to the end of the sky, but she focused on her first mission which was to save her neighbor, and indeed she managed to get her out safely from the woods, then they both landed on the ground.

Julia kept looking at the ground with shame and was unable to raise her face to look at the little girl until Sara said in sweet words just like her soul: It's okay, I forgive you and I do not even want an apology from you. My mom once taught me that envy does not come with any benefit and that we should never harm each other's, so let us all reconcile and move on with love and hearts full of good.

They smiled at the face of each other, and both of them went to their homes, and they learned a very important lesson.

Chapter 8:
A Weak Soul

U nicorn is nature-loving beings and is considered a symbol of peace and goodness. Still, just as any society, there are exceptions, just as there is love, there is hate, this applies to all societies, including unicorns.

There was a pernicious unicorn called Nathan, he had a weak soul and could be easily seduced, but unfortunately, he used to guard the town's borders, and he was supervising the town gate during the night.

His job was to prevent enemies from entering the town, He always intended to show honesty and goodness, and he continued to do so until a lousy day came for the whole town.

A herd of evil wolves was living alongside the town of unicorns; they envied them for their kindness and cooperation with each other, their society was somehow disjointed, they did not like to help each other or even those around them.

They wanted to steal the unicorn town, but they could not do that because guards were always there around the town, so that their leader once said: Unicorns are very solidarity, I have long looked for any way to steal their holdings, but I have never been able to, there is always a guard watching during the night, he stays standing there and never sleeps, I think his name is Nathan.

One day, one of his assistances came to him to present him with a new idea. Evil was visible on his face as he approached the leader and said: Why don't we give bribes to Nathan? We offer him a lot of money, and if he accepts, we will enter the town and steal everything in it. We will also tell him that he is safe, and we will not steal anything from him, and if he rejects our offer, we will not lose anything at all.

The leader liked the idea and asked his assistant to give him some time to think about it; after deep thinking, this evil idea convinced him.

The leader decided to implement the plan and called the assistant to agree on what they would specifically do; he said to him: Go to the guard with a bag full of pieces of gold and if he asked for more give him more, do not worry because what we are going to steal will be much more than that. Also, we will tell him that he is safe and that we will not steal anything from him. All he has to do is to open the gate for us so that we can all enter the town in the evening.

Indeed, the assistant went to Nathan and told him everything. At first, Nathan was worried and afraid of two things; first was the wolves and that they might harm him if he refused their request, second was the people of his town. If they discovered the matter, the unicorns would never forgive him for this betrayal.

He was hesitant and did not know what to do until the wolf brought him the money, he started tending to accept the wolves' request and then said: But the unicorns in the town will hate me, and they will be hurt, and I do not want that. They are my family and my friends, first of all.

The wolf looked at him with a sharp and frightening look, then took out more gold coins for him and said in bundles: Look at these gold coins, Nathan, they will all become yours. Also, no one will know that you are the one who allowed us to enter, and we will not harm or hit any of them, we will take what we need and just leave quietly, come on and I will give you more gold coins if you ask.

Nathan agreed to allow the wolves to enter the next evening, but only on the condition that they abide by the agreement that the wolf told him, and indeed the next day, a huge herd of wolves came and found the door open as they agreed with the guard.

They entered the city and stole almost all the houses, and they were carrying sticks to hit everyone who stood in their way, so they violated the agreement with the guard and harmed many unicorns. And not only that, but they went to Nathan's house and stole it and took the gold coins they had given him before,

64 | P a g .

to show later that all this agreement was just a lie so that they could harm the unicorns.

Panic spread among the town until the brave rescue squad came with their powerful wings, their sturdy legs, and hard horns. They were able to drive all the wolves out of town crying out: Get out, this is not your city, and this is not your wealth, go away, thieves.

They were also able to take back everything that the wolves stole, they returned the belongings to their owners, the situation was saved thanks to the courage and strength of the rescue squad, and no one of the unicorns lost his wealth.

The traitor guard felt ashamed of himself; he felt naive as the wolves deceived him and he was not smart enough to know that they were lying to him, he decided to tell them the truth and ask for forgiveness.

Nathan went to the unicorn who investigates the matter and said to him: I am the one who allowed them to enter, and I took some gold coins in exchange for that, I will give them to you as I will never take them, they told me that they would not harm anyone, but they have lied, and I was very fooled and did not realize that I am sorry and I hope all of you forgive me, I will never do it again.

The investigator unicorn said to him, and he began to pity him: We have saved the situation thanks to the courage of our soldiers, we will forgive you all, Nathan, for we forgive beings by nature, but let this be a lesson for you and everyone that betrayal only returns with consequences for everyone, and that trust in bad people and liars is a big mistake because they will lie to you to carry out their evil plans finally and harm you, your family and your friends.

The guard learned the lesson and became an example of honesty and courage; he returned to work guarding the city again and committed himself to his work to the fullest.

Chapter 9:
Good Sport

There was a lovely kingdom nestled in the hills to the west of Waxshire, known as Opal. The two communities were very friendly with one another, as they held many of the same values. The people of Opal were some of the most amiable that the princess had ever met.

The ruler of Opal was a man named Frederic. He refused to call himself a king because he believed the title to be regressive. Instead, he opted to be referred to only by his name. This decision caused some awkward exchanges during diplomatic visits to other kingdoms, as he was often referred to as "the Frederic of Opal."

He governed in an inherently different manner from the rest of the realm. He wanted to ensure than any ruler who came to power after him, could not subjugate his people. Frederic took power away from his own position and shared it with committees that he had formed based on the will of the people, through elections. He was a visionary, and one of King Ronald's closest friends.

Frederic was an eccentric man, but his unique spirit inspired the subjects of his domain. From Opal, came a slew of talented artists, thinkers, and musicians. The land was known to be a creative epicenter, seeing some of the most brilliant minds allowing their talent to grow beneath the peaceful ruler's reign.

One such artist was a woman named Maria. She was hailed far and wide as a creative mastermind. Her work spoke to a whimsical and childlike nature within the spirit of mankind. She painted visions of fairies and exotic magical lands. The entire realm sought out her commissions.

Princess Katie had been following Maria's career since she took up painting herself. The young woman looked up to the artist's technique. Maria managed to create some of the most realistic scenes of unrealistic subjects. The princess also related to the painter's vision of the world; she could see the magic in everything.

Princess Katie shrieked with excitement upon hearing that Maria would be visiting, along with a delegation from her own kingdom. She was even more pleased to hear that the painter's most renowned piece *Swan Beneath, a Full Summer Moon*, would be on display in Waxshire for the duration of her stay. The princess could hardly believe her ears when her father told her the news.

"That isn't all. There is more. You must promise me, though, that you aren't going to get worked up over what I am going to say next," the king said with a smile.

"I make no promises!" Katie said, excitedly awaiting his words.

"You know how proud the people of Opal are about their artistic abilities. Maria is sponsoring an art competition between Waxshire and Opal. The contestants will create whatever they want, using their chosen media. A panel of unbiased judges from a town to the west will declare a winner," King Ronald said.

"What is the prize?" Katie asked, her eyes widened by the news.

"*Swan Beneath a Full Summer Moon,*" said the king, wincing as he prepared for his daughter's scream. She did not disappoint. He explained that the winning kingdom would be allowed to keep the painting. All the citizens of Opal wanted it in their own castle, but Maria wanted them to earn it. The painter was passionate about inspiring others; hence, the competition was a result of this desire.

Princess Katie set to work immediately. She was going to practice until she had achieved a better level of detail. The young woman daydreamed that she might be the one responsible for winning the painting for Waxshire. She wanted to dominate the competition singlehandedly.

"Be careful," her unicorn friend warned her. She paced back and forth in front of him as they stood in the forest. The princess had disregarded entirely his words. Her mind was racing. The blue unicorn rolled his eyes, and she fidgeted about, brainstorming. "Don't be one of those people. They are the worst."

"What do you mean? One of what people?" She asked, finally struck by his voice.

"The people who are only interested in besting others. I get that she is an idol of yours but watch that impulse, or it is going to get you in trouble. I should know," Blue said. The princess was struck by the beauty of his pastel coat against the bleakness of the gray forest. The sky was overcast and full of clouds, and the air was becoming bitterly cold. The unicorn was the one colorful thing; he looked like a rip in reality. Katie considered making him the subject of her winning painting.

"I am not like you," she said, laughing.

"I have a weird midnight unity song that says you are incorrect, best friend," said the unicorn.

"Yeah, well, maybe magic isn't as all-knowing as the unicorns and fairies of the world would have us believe," the princess said, joking. She sat upon a damp log, realizing her mistake too late.

"This unicorn is still pretty human. All I am asking is that you keep your ambition in check. Make sure that you are out to create something lovely," he said.

"Of course, Blue. What else would I be doing?" she asked.

The princess practiced relentlessly. Her younger sister, Leah, was also entering the competition. Katie was slightly annoyed by Leah's choice to involve herself, as it was one more person that she was going to have to out-do.

Katie threw herself into the process. The princess began teaching herself new techniques and methods for achieving realistic detail. Brushstrokes became a serious focus for the young lady; she wanted to use them to tell her story. Katie loved painting but was allowing herself to become tightly wound; she was stressed out every moment that she was away from the canvas.

Leah was getting better too. The painting was more of a hobby for Leah, but she was leaning upon art for entertainment during the gloomy pre-winter haze. Roaming around outside was becoming less feasible as the days were growing cold and dark. The youngest princess used her imagination to transport her to warmer lands. She conveyed these scenes with her brush.

Katie was slowly learning to control her impulse for jealousy. The competition was not helping with that issue. She watched Leah seemingly effortlessly painting beaches and palm trees; she was angry with herself for not having the idea first.

The day of the competition arrived. The contestants were scattered around the ballroom. Some were sitting on the floor, working with mounds of wet clay; others stood beside their easels. They were going to be given five hours with which to craft their masterpieces.

Katie decided to paint a rainy autumn scene in the way that her unicorn friend had described it to her. She had never liked the cold, but he found beauty in the stoic nature of barren trees and gloomy skies. The princess was going to attempt to capture his vision of late autumn. She was going to add him to the center of the image, looking out to the viewers. In her humble opinion, her friend was the most beautiful creature. He would surely stand out in such muted earth tones.

The princess worked intently for hours. She carefully added excess paint and then swiped her brush across it to create the illusion of hair. His mane was her favorite thing part. It was so pale, but it looked to be dusted with crushed diamonds. It was a challenge to translate the shimmer into a painting; she loved a challenge.

Katie used a cream color for his mane, with a dash of sky-blue mixed in. She then added gray to the mixture to account for the shadows from the autumn rainclouds. The princess used random bursts of pastel to convey the glittering nature of his hair, and the iridescence of his horn.

In the end, Katie created an image of which she was proud of. The princess stared at her own work, finally able to conceptualize the magic in bleak rainy days. For her, it was that *bad,* which is necessary for the *good.* She did not see things quite the way Blue did, but it made perfect sense to Katie that she should appreciate the drear forest. How would she ever know the beauty of summer, if not for the cold contrast of winter?

Katie stood in a long line of artists as the winner was to be announced. The panel had walked slowly in front of all of the work that had been produced. This was the first time that the princess felt nervous, as though she perhaps wasn't good enough. There was so much talent in that room.

The winner was a young man from Opal who had sculpted a gallant knight in full armor. The judges unanimously adored his creation. Katie felt her heartbreaking within her chest when she realized that she was not going to be chosen. She quietly cried, embarrassed that she could not stop the tears from rolling down her cheek.

She was so proud of her painting. The princess did not understand how the judges were unable to see what she saw. Katie took a deep breath to compose her thoughts. She was disappointed in herself for not being good enough to catch the panel's attention.

There was to be a banquet in celebration of the competition. Everyone was jovial, chatting amongst themselves as they prepared for the feast. The princess smiled and bantered with the other contestants, congratulating the young man who won, for his success. He thanked the young lady for her kind words and introduced himself as Jon.

"I saw your painting. It was beautiful. I have always admired those who can find beauty in sadness. The lonely unicorn was a touching detail. Your work is enchanting," the young man said. He had seen something completely different than she had in her own work. She smiled, thinking of her mother's words about art being open to interpretation. The young man had kind eyes; she found herself feeling pleased that he had won. His sculpture was fascinating; the knight was a study in stoicism.

"I agree, you are both so talented," said a feminine voice from behind the pair. Katie froze, she recognized the tone. She turned to see her idol standing near her. Maria was so beautiful, up-close. "Princess, you remind me of myself at your age."

"T-thank you. I am such a fan, your work. You have inspired me to become a better painter," the princess said.

"You are welcome. I am actually starting a mentoring program for young artists, and I would like you both to come to a meeting if you would be interested. You guys are so important to the future," Maria said.

The princess was shocked. She was enthusiastically interested in Maria's offer and told her as much. The young man was also smiling uncontrollably. Katie was glad that she was not the only excited party in this exchange. Katie and Jon spent the duration of the banquet discussing the prospect. When she finally allowed herself to let go of her loss, everything began to turn around.

Chapter 10:
Where is your Mother?

L ong, long ago, there was a great, big nest filled up with lots of little, round eggs. The eggs were all quite smooth and hard and creamy in color, and they were all tucked gently between layers of leaves and feathers that had been gathered up. The mother of this nest of eggs was a maiasaura named Marcy, and Marcy loved her eggs. Like all Maiasaura, she was a perfect mother, and she loved to take care of her babies more than anything else. She loved trying to make sure that the nests that she had were perfect. She would clean it out and make sure that her babies would have everything that they would need when they all hatched.

One day, hatching day came around. First came a little maiasaura baby that she named Mia. Then, the others started to hatch, too. There were Millie and Mara, and Mike and Matt. And then, there was the egg in the middle of the nest that had not hatched at all.

"How strange!" Marcy said as she looked at all of her newly hatched babies and the one egg that had still not hatched. "It should be ready to hatch by now." She nudged the egg gently with her nose and then went back to tending to her babies that were already there. She fed them and got them comfortable and made sure that they were all ready to sleep when it was bedtime. Marcy brought all of her babies in nice and close when she curled up to sleep, and she made sure to keep that one last egg safe too.

When Marcy woke up that morning, she counted all of her babies. There were Mia and Millie. Mara and Mike were there, too. And there was Matt... And what was that?

Next to Matt, there was a strange dinosaur. It was brightly colored with strange feathers. It had a longer tail, and the head looked long and narrow, too. "What are you?" she asked quietly, nudging at the baby that had curled up with hers. When she looked over, she realized that the last egg in her nest must have hatched! This was what was inside of it!

"Weird!' said Marcy. "You're not one of my babies. You look like a raptor," she said, poking at the raptor's long toe. She looked around. Maybe he had rolled in form another nest, she thought, but then she remembered that other dinosaurs in the area were only other herbivores. The carnivores usually did not nest there near them.

"Oh, what am I going to do with you!"

Marcy looked at the baby that was curled up with her own. She thought that she could move him out of her nest and wait to see if his own mother found him, but that meant that he would have to sit out in the cold without anyone there to keep him warm. The thought of sending a baby out into the world without protection or without anyone there to help him was hurting. She didn't want to do that to him—in fact, she was quite certain that she just could not do that to him, even if she did want to.

"What if I ask around?" She thought that maybe if she told other dinosaurs that she had hatched a raptor, they could get the word out to everyone else too and see if any other dinosaurs were missing babies somewhere. But, then, she would have to tell other dinosaurs, mostly raptors, right where her nest was, and that didn't feel right, either!

Marcy sighed. "I guess I'll just have to take you over to the carnivore nesting ground myself then, won't I?" The baby dinosaur never even woke up to the sound of her talking. He just cuddled up to Mike and snored and snored.

Marcy smiled a bit to herself. She was not fond of raptors, but this one was definitely cute, and she could not deny that at all.

Later that morning, when all of the dinosaurs had woken up, she decided that it was time to go. She called for another maiasaura to watch her nest for her while she picked up the strange baby raptor and headed off. "Don't worry, little guy," she told him as she carried him. "We'll find your mama."

The baby looked up at her in confusion. "Aren't you my mama?" he asked her.

"No, I'm not, child. Look at your claws on your hands," she said. "Now, look at mine!" She lifted one of her front legs to show the hooves that she used to walk around. "Look at your feet—see those claws? I don't have claws like that."

The raptor looked at his feet and saw the claws and nodded his head. "I get it," he said. "I'm different. But that's okay!"

Marcy nodded. "That is okay! But, we have to get you back to your mother. I'm sure that she is worried sick." So, off they went to go searching for the raptor's mother. They first stopped near the beach. There was usually a nest or two of raptors there every summer, Marcy knew, but that summer, the beach was empty. When she looked around, there were no real places there that someone could have nested. "Not here," she said sadly as she kept ongoing.

The raptor rode on her shoulder as they went from place to place, hunting down the right nest for him. She kept on trucking along, looking all over. "You know, I think they like to nest near the marsh, too."

So, off they went to the marsh> When she got there, she asked a nice pachycephalosaurus if she knew of any raptor's nests around there.

"Nope, none here," she replied, looking at the strange sight. It wasn't normal to see a little raptor hanging onto a maiasaura.

Marcy sighed and nodded her head. "Thanks anyway," she told the pachycephalosaurus before heading off for the next place to look. They had to be around there somewhere! It was just a matter of figuring out where to go, and Marcy was not willing to give up yet.

So, they went off into the jungle. Marcy asked every single dinosaur they passed if they knew of any raptors, but they all shook their heads no in response. No one knew where to find a raptor that had lost an egg, and Marcy was beginning to feel very bad for the poor little guy. He was very cute and very cuddly, but he needed a home, and Marcy thought that his home would be best with other dinosaurs that understood him better.

Marcy eventually sighed and settled down on the ground for a little break. "I don't know if we'll find your mama," she said sadly to the little raptor.

"That's okay, Mama!" he replied, snuggling up against Marcy's neck. "You're nice anyway. I like you!"

Marcy smiled a little bit. She felt bad, but there was nothing that she would be able to do. The best that she really could do was just take him home. The only other alternative that she saw at that point in time, having not been able to find a raptor anywhere that she went, was just to leave him there, stranded in the middle of the jungle, but that did not seem fair at all.

Without seeing another option that made sense, Marcy sighed. "I like you, too," she said with a smile, nuzzling the little raptor. "You might just have to come home with me."

"Yay!" the raptor exclaimed. "I wanted to do that anyway!"

"You did?" Marcy was surprised to hear that. "Why?"

"Because you're my mama," he replied.

Marcy stared at him in surprise. Maybe he was right, after all, she thought. He had hatched in her nest. He had slept with her babies. He had grown in that egg cuddled up against her in her nest, and he knew her sounds, her smells, and her voice. Maybe he was her baby, after all.

Marcy smiled at him and nodded her head. "Maybe I am your mama, my dear boy," she told him. Truthfully, she had not wanted to send him away from her anyway! She thought that he would be better off with a meat-eating dinosaur who would be able to teach him how to hunt and how to eat what he needed to live, but she was sure that she could find a way to do that, too.

So, Marcy brought him home with her. She decided to raise him as if he were her own, and he was. He may not have been borne from her body, but he was certainly grown in her heart, just like her other babies. He may have been different in some ways, but she could get past that. They were different, but they were the same, too. They both had the same two eyes. They both had mouths for eating. They had hearts for living and for loving. That was enough for her.

All of the other dinosaurs thought that it was strange. They were worried that, when the raptor started to grow up, he would try to eat them, but Miles, the raptor, learned not to do that. He learned to understand that they were not food—they were friends. He learned that if he wanted to eat, there were non-dinosaur options that he could find that would be just fine without having to eat another dinosaur, and he learned that they tasted good, too.

So, Miles, the raptor, grew up with all maiasaura siblings. He grew longer and featherier while his brothers and sisters all grew larger and larger. It didn't' take long until he was the smallest one in the nest! And that was okay, for he knew that even if he was the smallest one in the nest, he had a big share of his mother's heart.

Marcy learned that she did not have only to love those that looked like her or acted like her. She learned that differences were beautiful and that family could be chosen instead of just being born. The longer that she raised Miles, the more serious she felt about that idea. She loved him more and more with each passing day, and even though she knew that someday, he would have to leave and go off on his own, she knew that time was not yet, and she knew that she could enjoy the time that she still had while raising him.

Chapter 11:
A Sticky Situation

A llen, the ankylosaurus, had a very spiky back, and he had the personality to match, too. He was not a very kind dinosaur. He liked to make other dinosaurs upset or angry, and he would do his best to annoy them whenever he had the chance. He loved to bother other dinosaurs if he could, and he loved to watch them get annoyed. It made him happy to know that he could bully others and bother them. It made him feel like he was stronger than them, even if he was smaller and slower. But, most other dinosaurs did not like him because of this. They hated how mean he could be, and they hated to be around him whenever they had no other choice.

One day, Allen was out at the watering hole. He was drinking up the water quietly, watching as some other dinosaurs had some fun around them. They were talking about how they were going to take an adventure to the nearby beach to have some fun for the day, but Allen had other plans for them. He wanted them to feel as annoyed and grumpy as he did instead of having fun, so he knew that he had to do something—and quick. So, he stood up, turned away from the water, and looked right at them.

He could see Alex the apatosaurus and the triceratops sisters, Trina and Trixie. They were all talking excitedly with each other. "You know," Allen said loudly as he looked at the other dinosaurs. "It's only a good time when you don't always have to slow down for someone else." He looked right at Alex, who was quite a bit slower than Trina and Trixie. After all, it was very hard to run about when you have to balance out a very long neck!

Trina and Trixie looked at each other in confusion, and then they looked right back at Allen. "Okay?" they asked, uncertain what his point was.

"So, if you want actually to be able to enjoy most of your day, ditch the dope and find someone that can move quicker." Allen grinned as he saw Alex look upset. Alex looked down at his friends sadly, hoping that they would not decide to leave him behind.

"Why would we do that?" asked Trixie.

"Yeah! We like Alex!" said Trina. They were not very happy with the attitude that Allen had, and they were not afraid to show it. They wanted to make him realize that they were not going to let him ruin their beach time adventure! So, the three dinosaurs turned away and left.

This made Allen quite angry. They weren't allowed to walk away like that! So, he decided that he would follow them and make them even angrier at the beach. Off he went with his little, stubby legs, but before he could get very far, they had disappeared. After all, they were far quicker than he was, and they were far better at walking with longer legs than he was.

But, before long, that didn't matter anymore. Allen found someone else to bother. He saw Rocco the stegosaurus eating at some leaves. Rocco kept making funny faces as he nibbled on everyone, little by little. It looked like he was searching for something, but he was not finding whatever it was that he wanted. Allen grinned, moving up to the stegosaurus. He was ready for his newest target! "If you keep making faces like that, it'll get stuck. But who knows, maybe that would be an improvement from what it is right now!" the ankylosaurus laughed and laughed at his joke, but Rocco frowned.

"Do you want something?" he asked without even looking at the dinosaur. He just kept on moving about, searching for the perfect plant for his lunch.

"Yeah. I want you to grow up," said Allen. "You know, you're just wasting all of those other leaves when you eat them. What a fool! Just eat the food and be done with it! Or is that too much to ask for your little nut-sized brain to handle?"

"Your brain is quite nut-sized, too, thank you," Rocco replied without missing a beat. He couldn't be bothered to care that the dinosaur was going up and down, bothering him. He was so used to being bothered about his eating habits that it didn't even matter to him anymore. He was completely content simply being himself and simply enjoying his food his way.

Allen scowled. "What's wrong with you?" he asked Rocco before stomping off to be by himself. He was so annoyed that no one was getting annoyed by him! But, everyone else was so used to him bothering them and bullying them that they didn't even listen to what he had to say anymore. They simply ignored him and moved on, and they had been doing so all day.

So, off Allen stomped angrily. He might not have been able to bother the others, but he sure could stomp his feet and bother the ground instead! He stomped and stomped, too busy thinking about how annoyed he was actually to pay attention to where he was going... And he got stuck! Suddenly, he realized that he could not lift his feet anymore. He was stuck in the mud, and there was nothing that he could do about it!

He pulled and pulled. He tugged and tugged. But, he was stuck tight. He looked all around him and realized that he was actually starting to sink into the mud—and he couldn't get out! "Help!" he cried out. "Help me!" He tried and tried to move, but the more he struggled, the deeper he sank.

Soon, drawn by the sounds of yelling, Alex, Trina, and Trixie came to investigate. They saw Allen stuck in the mud and looked at each other. "What should we do?" asked Trina.

"I vote we leave the grump there," said Trixie with a smirk.

Allen felt his heart sink. "Please help me," he asked them.

"Why should we?" asked Trixie. "You're always so mean to us!"

"I know I am... I'm sorry!" Allen looked up at them. "I don't want to be stuck in the mud forever! Please help me get out of here!"

Alex sighed. "We can't just leave him there." He looked down at the ankylosaurus. "I'm not sure how we'll get him out, but we can't just try to do anything. We owe it to him and ourselves to at least do that much. We can do something if we really put our minds to it. We just have to try!"

Allen felt a bit better. "I'm sorry, guys... I won't be so mean again! I swear it!" He realized that he was very lucky that they were willing to help after he had been so mean to all of them. He was mean to just about everyone even though he really shouldn't be, and he just couldn't help it or himself. But, he knew that if he got out of this mess, he would have to try his hardest to get along better with everyone. If they helped him out, he had to learn how to stop being mean to everyone.

"What if we tried pulling him out by his tail?" asked Trina. She was eyeing his big, clubbed tail carefully, staying back so it would not accidentally hit her.

"We could try…" said Alex. "What do you say, Allen?" He didn't want to pull Allen's tail without asking first.

"Do whatever you gotta do—just get me out of here!" Allen replied. He felt the mud getting higher up on his back, and he was getting really nervous.

"Can you feel the bottom of the mud pit?" asked Trixie as Alex moved behind Allen to grab and pull on his tail.

"No, I can't," said Allen, really starting to worry.

"That's okay, we'll have you out of there soon anyway!" said Alex as he lowered his head and grabbed onto his tail. "Hang on—this might hurt a bit." Alex pulled as hard as he could, but nothing happened. Allen was stuck tight!

"Ow!" Allen cried out as Alex pulled and pulled. Alex let go with a sigh. "That's not working.

Alex looked around. "I don't know how we're going to get you out of here…" he said quietly.

But then, Rocco appeared. He looked around at everyone. "What's going on?" he asked with a confused expression as he looked over the situation. That did not look safe at all, but he was not sure that there was really anything that he could do to help.

"Allen is stuck," said Alex with a sigh. "Any ideas on getting him out?"

Rocco stared at Allen for a long, hard minute. "No, sorry. My nut-brain is too small."

Alex, Trina, and Trixie stared at Rocco in confusion.

"I'm sorry!" Allen cried out sadly. "I'm sorry I'm such a bully! I'm sorry I say such mean things! Please just help me get out of here, and I'll never do it again, I promise!"

Rocco sighed. He didn't feel right just leaving Allen stuck there, even if Allen had been cruel. He felt like he owed it to himself to at least try to get him out. So, Rocco looked around and thought about the situation. "What if we used a big stick underneath him and pried him out?"

Everyone looked at Rocco in shock. That was a perfect idea! So, they went to work, looking for great, big sticks that they could use. The sticks had to be very wide across so that they would hold up Rocco's big body. When they all found some, they brought them back to the mud pit. Each dinosaur was holding large branches that they could use. They were all pushed underneath Rocco, one by one, until they each had their own leverage. Then, on the count of three, each of them pushed down on their branches with all of their weight...

And Rocco was coming free! Little by little, they were getting him out of the mud, and soon, he was completely out, and they carefully walked backward together with him still stuck on the branches. They let him go when they got him above the ground again, and he looked up at all of them. "Thank you for helping me," he told them all. "I promise I'll try to do better so that I don't keep hurting you all the time."

"Good!" Trina snapped. "Because you're not fun to be around at all."

"I'm only like that because you guys never want to hang out with me..." said Allen sadly.

"We only don't want to be around you because you're so mean," added in Trixie.

So, from then on, they had a deal with each other. Allen was kinder to them and stopped always trying to say things to make them angry. And, they all would regularly invite Allen along to play their games, too. They knew that Allen was really just lonely and that they would be able to help him feel more at home and more welcome if they were kinder, so they all tried their best, too, and they became great friends.

Conclusion

Preparing your children for bed and winding down the same way every single night is a great way to let your body know it is time to sleep. Do you know why that is? The answer is: routine!

Moment by Moment, Ever-Changing

Mindfulness takes practice. You may need to work on it as you would any other skill.

A soccer player practices footwork. A dancer trains muscles. A mathematician solves problems step by step. You cannot master your mind without practicing MINDFUL ME skills every day.

Meditation is staying alert and resting your mind in its calm, relaxed, and natural state.

So, remember, mindfulness is a choice. Your choice. Being a MINDFUL ME is about connecting the dots between feeling an emotion, thinking a thought, and acting on them. It is about using meditation to train your mind and expand your heart.

Without mindfulness, you might react quickly to your thoughts and feelings, and do something you'll wish you hadn't. With mindfulness, you can find your way to your WISDOM MIND, which is open, accepting, and generous. Everything in the world changes from one minute to another. That's true for your thoughts and feelings too. If you were distracted a minute ago, remember that minute is over. You have another chance to be mindful in this present moment. With each new breath, you can pay attention.

Your body and mind love having the same hints that it is time to do something like eat or go to sleep. When you take the time to make your sleep routine a habit, your body and mind begin to learn that this routine means it is time to go to sleep.

As you continue to repeat the habit and see these benefits, you will find yourself having a much better sleep every single night. Plus, it will become much easier for you to fall asleep because you are actually tired and ready for a good rest. This means that when waking up, you will be ready to enjoy plenty of great fun with your friends and family all over again!

Lastly, if you enjoyed all of the stories in this book, tell other kids about these wonderful stories and enjoy falling asleep to them, just like you!

Thank you, and I wish you many wonderful dreams. Goodnight!

CPSIA information can be obtained
at www.ICGtesting.com
Printed in the USA
BVHW081657260221
601199BV00009B/991